Where do balloons LAND?

JILL CLARK

ILLUSTRATED BY
VIVIAN SAAD

Published by Taylor and Seale Publishing, LLC.

Acknowledgements

Mary Custureri, Taylor and Seale Publishing, *Where Do Balloons Land?*   2022

Wright Elementary School students for asking about the stories behind
       select poems in the *Loose Balloons'* book, which gave rise
       to the idea in *Where Do Balloons Land?*   2021

"Okra," Shannon Morgan [Activity Section]   2021

"My Little Green Truck," *The Writers Club*, GreyThoughts Publishing   2021

"Old Germs," musical score by Steliana Hindalova   2021

"Missouri Summer Nights," *The Poet*, Publisher Robin Barratt   2021

"Who Am I?" *The Poet*, Publisher Robin Barratt   2021

"The Black-Capped Chickadee," *The Poet*, Publisher Robin Barratt.
       Illustrator, Vivian Saad, *Where Do Balloons Land?*   2020

"The Black-Capped Chickadee," *Bumples Interactive Online Magazine*,
       Publisher Jennifer Sheehan   2020

"Turkey Jamboree," *Creativity Webzine*, Publisher Charles Moulton.
       Illustrator, Brandy Winston, *Where Do Balloons Land?*   2020

"Vampire Treats," Original Illustrator: Brandy Winston. *Neighbors
       Magazine*, Publisher Don Pritchett. Katelyn Albrycht,
       Content Coordinator   2020

"My Cousin's Drawings," *PKA's Advocate Publication*, Publisher Patricia Keller   2019

"Missouri Summer Nights," *Celestial Musings*, Stacy Savage Compiler   2018

"West Indian Manatee," *Vanishing from Waterways*, Carol-Rhoda Publisher
       [Lerner Publications Endangered Species *Vanishing* Series]   2001

"Missouri Summer Nights," *The Independent Review*   1998

Dedication

To Anna Schranz for her loving support and friendship.

To Dr. Joseph Siry for passing on his environmental devotion.

To Shannon Morgan for modeling how families should love one another.

To my husband John Clark whose intuitive wit, not unlike the Fairy's dust, sprinkled its way into each poem.

To our grandchildren who have served as fonts of childhood imagination and fun.

To Chip Slaughter for his original, droll concepts that breathed the first breath of reality into the idea for a book.

To our children Ryan, Patria and Jenny for keeping the light of hope on at night.

To Trey Williams who strives to walk the path of God.

To Mary Custureri for making literary wishes come true.

To Dr. Anita Gail Choice whose love provides educationally fun reading opportunities for children.

To Vivian Saad whose illustrations ignite character depth and interpretive meaning.

To Brandy Winston whose sassy and clever ideas dance through her drawings.

To my siblings – Patrick, Shannon, Molly and Kevin whose creativity is as varied as the stars.

Introduction

Where Do Balloons Land? completes the second book in the *Loose Balloons Series*. This book is for children ages 8-14, and some of the same characters have grown up — in the same way as the children who have read about and followed the characters from the maiden book *Loose Balloons*. For example, in the poem "The Wind" from the first book, do you recognize the character who is flying a kite as he reappears in *Where Do Balloons Land?*

I included in this book the initial poems "Frog's the Name" and "Toad's Retort" from the start in the series for those who may not have read *Loose Balloons*. The illustrator of the second book Vivian Saad imagined and futurized Frog and Toad with her ideas in relation to what these two rascals might look like aged-up. Her drawings moved me to tears.

The illustrator for *Loose Balloons* Brandy Winston interpreted Frog and Toad with a unique attitude that brought these rivaling amphibians to battle.

Chip Slaughter's early artwork gave birth to Frog and Toad. His drawings injected the primordial living tissue into these ectothermic tetrapod vertebrates whose personalities had, up until that point, only swum aimlessly in my head.

Frog and Toad illustrations by Chip Slaughter

First Edition published by
Taylor and Seale Publishing, LLC.
Daytona Beach Shores, Florida
Copyright © 2022 by Jill Clark. All rights reserved.
ISBN: 978-1-950613-99-1

Taylor and Seale Publishing, LLC.
3408 S. Atlantic Avenue, Unit 139
Daytona Beach Shores, Florida 32118
mk@taylorandseale.com
1-386-760-8987

Taylor and Seale books are available at the following:

Amazon.com
Amazon Kindle
Barnes and Noble
Books-A-Million
Taylor and Seale Publishing, LLC.
and in numerous other bookstores

To buy in bulk for schools, museums, and organizations, please contact
Taylor and Seale Publishing for special discounts
mk@taylorandseale.com

Lesson Plans for *Where Do Balloons Land?* available at
www.jillswriterscafe.com

Contents

OUTDOORSY

INDOORSY

HOLIDAYZIE

ONE FOR THE ROAD

APPENDICES A,B,C

APPENDIX A-CREATIVITY TWISTERS

OUTDOORSY

FROG'S THE NAME

Some people call me tree toad
but really I'm a frog.
My suction feet can grip a tree
as well as any log.
My skin is moist and shiny,
you'll barely feel a bump.
I sit on lily pads in ponds,
(most toads prefer a stump).
My eyes so bulge with beauty,
you'd know them anywhere,
with frog's legs as a diner's treat,
I guard them with great care.
So if you hear me called a toad,
remember my true name:
Frogs aren't toads, and toads aren't frogs,
we're really not the same.

TOAD'S RETORT

I'd heard it all when I heard that frog
boasting he could grip a log.
Those suction feet he flaps around
would only prove to slow me down.
He croaks all day on a lily weed;
a quiet stump is all I need.
My beauty bumps hold water in;
a toad must have his pond to swim.
But on one point I will agree:
Don't confuse that frog with me,
I'm nothing like my slimy mate,
whose legs look scrumptious on your plate!

FROG'S STILL THE NAME

All I did was make the claim
that toads and frogs are not the same,
but that toad served up my legs to eat
on a diner's plate for human treat!

How dare he call me slimy skin:
My lustrous sheen soaks water in.
In ponds I frolic leapfrog high.
My sticky tongue can catch a fly.

How tiresome to sit all the day.
On a wooden stump
I hop and play.

But on one point, I will agree,
don't confuse that toad with me,
whose barnacled bumps
so proud protrude –
attracting snakes
to toady food.

TOAD'S RE-RETORT

He who laughs last,
laughs best I've heard,
that's because retorts
have the final word.
To a cacophonous croaker
who could wake the dead,
for once and all,
I'll lay frog's claims to bed:
No need for me to jump or leap,
to lose my dignity or beauty sleep.
The bugs line up for me to taste,
the honor's all theirs; no need for haste.
My poise commands a quiet calm.
Who needs such boisterous froggy song?
My exotic bumps shine flecks of gold—
a royal trait of ages old.

You may have forgotten, my slithery friend,
we're related species and to that end,
I'll ask you to honor
the amphibians we be....

A toad is really a kind of frog,
and since you like to hop and jump,
I'll scoot over...
so we can share a stump.

THE CENTIPEDE

The centipede
moves at a speed
fast with feathery feet.
Some live in people's houses
to bask in dark, warm heat.
Some hide outdoors in logs
waiting for their prey—
an ant perhaps or spider
happening by the way.
The centipede does NOT possess
a hundred crawly feet,
but rather a mere sixty
shuffle briskly down the street.

centipede: n. an arthropod with predatory segments of legs, of which the front pair contain poisonous teeth-like structures or fangs

THE SHY RAINBOW SNAKE

The rainbow snake once feared extinct,
hides in the day just like the mink:
One you'll see, the other not.

The rainbow snake prefers the water,
just like the playful, friendly otter:
One you'll see, the other not.

The rainbow snake stays out of sight
invisible in the pale moonlight
weaving red and yellow stripes:
The moon you'll see, the snake you'll not.

rainbow snake: n. the rare subspecies from South Florida *Farancia erytrogramma seminola* inspired the poem

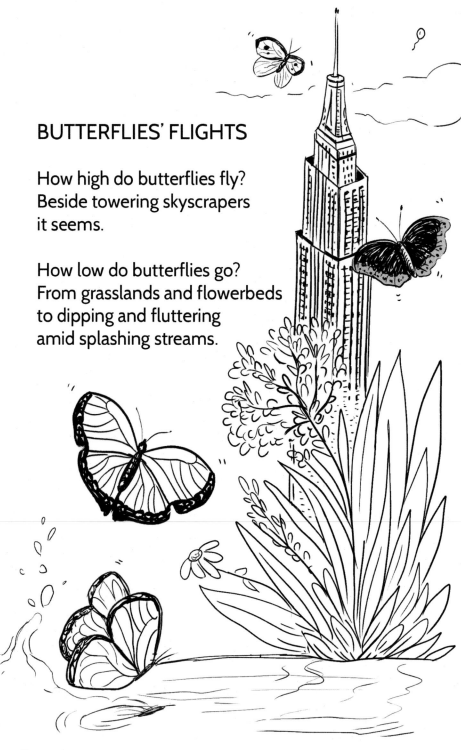

BUTTERFLIES' FLIGHTS

How high do butterflies fly?
Beside towering skyscrapers
it seems.

How low do butterflies go?
From grasslands and flowerbeds
to dipping and fluttering
amid splashing streams.

DO NOT!

Do not tickle a laughing hyena,
it will not laugh.
Do not tell a fib to a lion,
he likes the truth.
Do not feel the whiskers of a platypus,
she does not have whiskers.
And whatever you do,
do not play
in the sand of a red anthill,
unless, of course,
you want your fill
of ouches
and stings
and hops
and screams
and bites and hurts
and bumps and welts.
Then it is still NOT OKAY
to stomp and play
in the sand
of a red anthill.

hyena: n. a powerful, large meat-eating mammal not from the Americas and who usually scavenges for food

platypus: n. a carnivorous, small egg-laying aquatic mammal of eastern Australia and Tasmania that has a fleshy duck-like bill with webbed feet, dense fur, and a flattened tail

THE CACTUS FLOWER

A cactus blooms
a lovely flower,
but then again
its real power
rests
in its mighty sting.

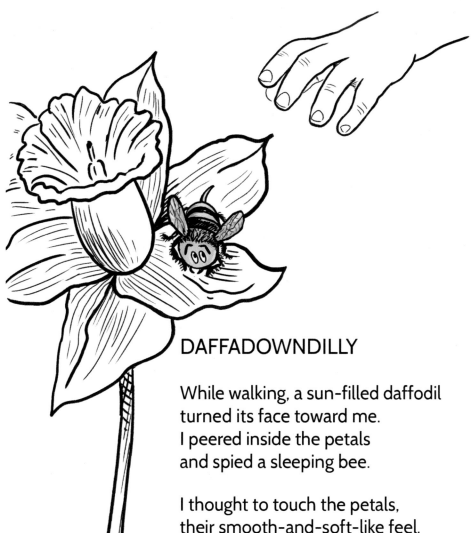

DAFFADOWNDILLY

While walking, a sun-filled daffodil
turned its face toward me.
I peered inside the petals
and spied a sleeping bee.

I thought to touch the petals,
their smooth-and-soft-like feel.

But then that weary bee
tired from pollinating,
being buffeted by the wind,
might want to test its stinger
on my soft-and-smooth-like skin.

daffodil: n. various bulbous herbs of the flower family amaryllis, particularly those that have a large crown stretched into a trumpet-like shape and that appear or grow year after year
buffeted: v. blown around

FIDDLE DEE DEE

Fiddle dee dee
look at me
flying a balloon like a kite.
What I don't understand—
just where it will land?
Or will it continue in flight?

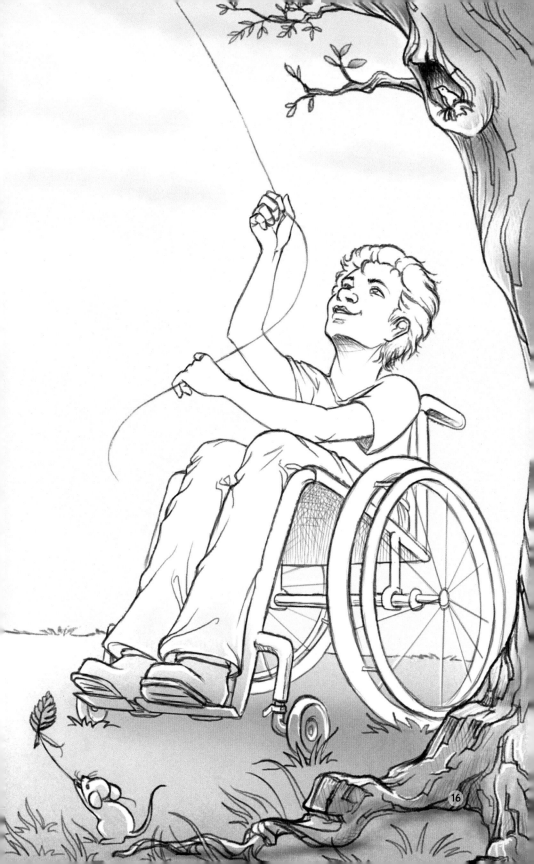

PROSPECTOR SON

The prospector son
consumed his life
digging for a treasure.
A pot of gold, a ruby ring,
other's praise and pleasure.
He noticed
not
his mother's smile
she treasured just for him.
Since
he could not
weigh it,
spend it,
or display it,
he found
not
his precious gem.

STORY CLOUDS

Clusters of cloud faces
float beneath God's wings;
whitish tuffs suspended
from imaginary strings.

Sky dividers
eclipsing
the earth from Heaven's eyes,
quenching terra-cotta's thirst
in precipitation cries.

See Apollo arching?
Billows of traveling strength
aiming at elusive Zeus,
with hair of Samson's length.

Far below these mighty fluffs
children's minds get caught
on stories only clouds tell
to winds that chase them off.

terra-cotta: n. a tannish-orange clay used in its natural state or glazed

STORMY WEATHER

Stormy weather does not scare me.
I like to hear
sky's Thunder Voice
announcing pelts of rain.
Gray clouds cry out
pent-up tears,
although they feel no pain.

Stormy weather sounds
mean-angry
with booming flares of power,
but sometimes Mother Nature
just needs to take a shower.

THE QUIET CLOUD

A solitary cloud
pushed past an angry wind,
the cloud looked back longingly
to its blustery friend.

"When you find yourself in calmer skies,"
the cloud was heard to say,
"would you tell me why you're mad at me?
I miss you every day.
You rush me around —
rain pelting through my mist.
The truth is I just float here
without your windy wisp.
I do not have a lot of friends,
it's hard for me to speak,
the sky can be a lonely place
for one so mild and meek."

"I don't know what comes over me,"
the wind whooshed 'round and 'round,
"sometimes I fear my strength
will falter to the ground.
I lose my gentle breezes,
I wrestle with my force,
if I understood it better,
I would choose a different course."

"I'll wait you out again then friend,"
the cloud hung timid by,
"I will love you through your windstorms
as you love me quiet and shy."

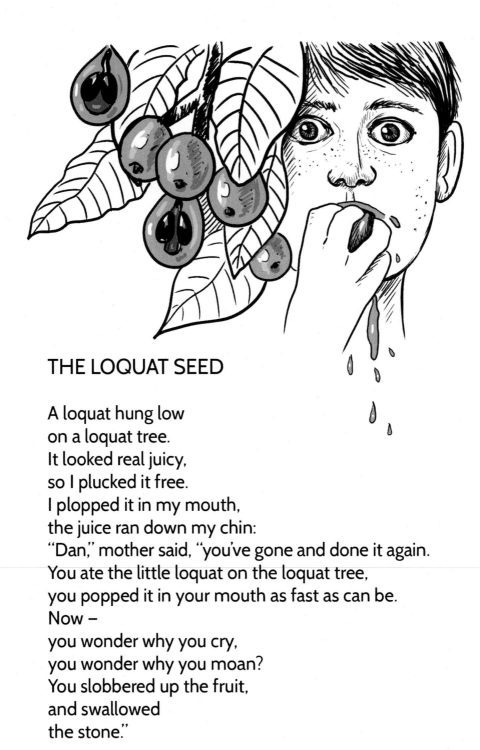

THE LOQUAT SEED

A loquat hung low
on a loquat tree.
It looked real juicy,
so I plucked it free.
I plopped it in my mouth,
the juice ran down my chin:
"Dan," mother said, "you've gone and done it again.
You ate the little loquat on the loquat tree,
you popped it in your mouth as fast as can be.
Now –
you wonder why you cry,
you wonder why you moan?
You slobbered up the fruit,
and swallowed
the stone."

CLOUD CHASE

Bright-white clouds turn golden in the sun.
I stretch to touch the floating fluff,
I jump and hop to tag the sky,
but clouds have wings,
and away they fly....

WISHING-STAR WAIT

If you wish upon a star,
remember that the star is far
away...
and know the wish you make
may take a loooooooooooooooo
ooooooooooooooooooooooooooooooooooooo
ooooooooooooooooooooooooooooooooooo
ooooooooooooooooooooooooooooooooo
ooooooooooooooooooooooooooooooooo
ooooong
time
to be heard.

But once that star
hears your wish,
that wish will be granted,
forthwith.

forthwith: adv. immediately; spontaneously

THE HIDING PLACE

A mask may shield a face of pain,
when you don't feel like laughing.
A mask helps you pretend in fun,
but then again, sometimes
it holds the hurt in.
A mask might turn your nose up
and make you feel superior,
but when that mask slips from your face,
you're bound to feel inferior.
A mask may make you feel quite safe
when tucked inside your hiding place.

One thing a mask will never do
is allow you to be
the real
you.

WHO AM I?

I stand a little shorter than my classmates do,
but I am me
and you are you.
When I throw a baseball,
I wince and make a face,
the ball spins 'round and 'round
and drops in place.
I don't run fast or dribble
a basketball well,
though in playful dance,
I do excel.

I know the kids who need a friend,
they are just like me—
shyer than the average kid
but who LOVE to see
sunsets through the clouds as we listen
to the waves.
We talk about the planets and explore
hidden caves.
Rock-hunting in the mountains
promises as much fun,
as watching my good friend
make a homerun.
I love to hear my friend
thwack a grand slam,
I love me, too,
for who I am.

HOW TO HANDLE A BULLY

Tick Tock Bullies knocked, I answered not the door.
Tick Tock they slunk away, but then came back for more.
Tick Tock the Bully socked and tried to push me down.
Tick Tock my chest puffed out: Staunch I stood my ground.
Tick Tock the Bully scoffed and called me ugly names.
Tick Tock I smiled inside–ignored the ugly games.
Tick Tock my Bully mocked my clothes and lovely face.
Tick Tock I danced away with confidence and grace.
Tick Tock my heart took stock in words my Bullies said:
Tick Tock I swam and drew and hiked outside instead.
Tick Tock the Bullies hid in corners unsuspecting.
Tick Tock I walked amid the rays of sun reflecting.
Tick Tock they Cyber-stalked to bully me online.
Tick Tock to leave or move, there also comes a time.
Tick Tock my Bully warned my silence is a must.
Tick Tock I shared my plight with those whom I could trust.

staunch: n. steadfast in loyalty or principle (in this case, respect of, and loyalty to, oneself)

HAPPY ENDING

I followed the yellow brick road,
I did just as I was told.
When I came to the end,
I started again,
since I found that the start
was really the end,
so I followed around
again and again.
And finally sat down
on the Finish Line
(that was painted next to the Start Sign).
And I said to myself,
I can't find the end –
because the end ends where the sign says it starts.
I must be LOST.
But, am I lost at the start, or lost at the end?
That is the question for you my friend.

Just remember the gold-paved
yellow brick road
is rarely where
you have been told.

Try to find your own way,
when a path you must take,
so you'll know where you start,
you'll know when you're through,
and better yet,
you'll know that person
that you call
you.

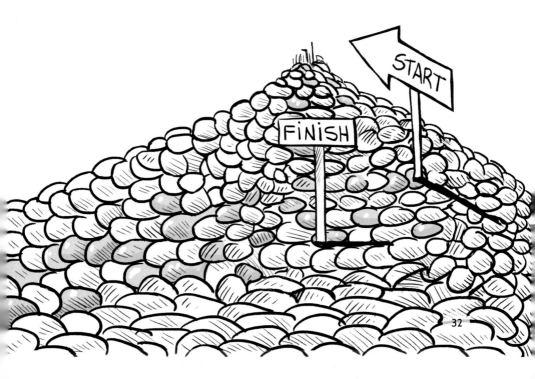

INDOORSY

GROWING UP

Gazing down on Sister Tess,
I see her little toddler's mess,
as Mother fondly pats her head,
still cherishing her unmade bed.
Her footprints on my dusty shelf?
Just puddin' toes of sister-elf.
I mess the place, it's not the same,
too big for cute, but not for blame.
My fingerprints on painted walls
won't bring the smiles like baby's paws.
I remember when I stuttered sweet,
lisped just to give my mom a treat.
"Poor grammar" now I sometimes hear,
from rich to poor in just a year.

Go back I wish...
just one more time,
recite that jumbled nursery rhyme,
feel Mom caress my waiting cheek,
hold fast her kiss that time won't keep.

OLD TOY CAR

Red race car tossed aside,
remember how my hands would glide
along your silver-streamlined pipes,
plump fingers trailing racing stripes.
Commanding you to stay on track,
sprinting off, but always back.
Black-checkered flag sailing free,
Gold Victory Cup just for me.
Now?
Shined winner's cup scratched and peeled
resting near your cracked windshield.
Your memory will not grow old
though cast aside, cast in gold.

FAIRY DUST

Flecks of stars and fairies' wings
flutter through the night.
The fairy's wand is dancing
and playing with the light.

If you hear the fairy sing,
as dreamy children do,
she's come to sprinkle
her sweet sleep
upon the likes of you.

MY COUSIN'S DRAWINGS

Each day I wait for the mail;
I hope there's a letter for me.
Sometimes I write to my cousin Kai.
He draws me pictures of the sea.
He creates chestnut-colored horses
cantering along the shore.
I like to write him story-poems
about King Arthur's Knights of Yore.
When I hear that mail truck rumble,
I gallop as fast as I can —
"Oh," I smile as I open Kai's picture
of King Arthur on an auburn mare,
as he gazes upon the deep-blue sea
with his horse,
his sword,
and his lady fair.

38

ARMPIT SQUISHY

I cup my hand over my armpit,
flapping the other arm
up and down....
I wonder if I could fly like this?
But instead–
hear a burping sound.

squishy: adj. the state of being damp and soft and pliant

CHIPMUNK CHEEKS

"Please, don't talk with your mouth full,"
I heard my Auntie say.
So...
I chewed and scrunched
and smacked and packed
and tucked my food away.

"You still have food in your mouth,"
Sister Beth was heard to shout:
So...
I munched and ground,
and crunched and found
my cheeks POPPED out!

SLIPPERY SUE

I have a playful sister,
her name is Sally Sue.
She likes to sip on soap suds
and slide around in goo.
She slaps and smacks the bubbles,
and pops them with her tongue,
my zany, crazy sister
so silly and so fun.

THE EVERYWHERE GOES NOSE

Bump, thump!
Smack a swinging door.
Shove the waiter by mistake,
sweep the restaurant floor.
Flip the soda fountain twice,
soda mixed in tea.
It's tough eating with a nose
big enough for three.
Smack and shatter window panes
with just a sideward look,
turn to tip the server,
flatten some poor cook.
I never do complain,
or scream or cry or munch,
since every time I sit to eat,
my nose whiffs up my lunch.

THE MUSHY GREEN BEAN

Never mess with a stringy green bean.
Pick the one with the waxy sheen.
Or the string will get caught in your throat–
you'll burp up and throw up and bloat.
These beans overcooked
pack a tasteless punch.
Beware if you find one
in your lunch.
They hang out with onions sassy and bold
(and onions make you cry I'm told).
You'll find these green beans
all gunked
in mushroom stew,
then glopped in casseroles
just for you.

BUT
if you find fresh beans
with strings of seed pods,
you can say to yourself,
Wow!
What are the odds?
These beans are not bland
or boring
or hollow–
I can snap 'em and crunch 'em
and now–
I can swallow.

gunked: v. author's poetic license

JIMMY DEFY-YA

Jimmy Defy-Ya
the boy to try ya,
just when you try
to be nice.
You give him a smile,
he sticks out his tongue,
and then insults you
twice.
The teacher asks Jimmy,
"Please go wash your hands."
But he walks on his hands instead.
When he gets to the bathroom,
what does he do?
He paints his elbows red.
He goes to the dentist – Dr. McHill,
for four huge cavities,
he needs to fill.
The dentist warns Jimmy,
"Don't eat for one hour –
let your fillings set."
But his cheek is numb,
and he's hungry by gum,
so he bites a hole
in his cheek
in regret.

Now,
Jimmy sings much better
than he ever did,
with a cheek
that can whistle along;
but he sings during class
and whistles alas
to create an aeolian song.

aeolian: adj. caused by the wind

RIGAMAROLE RAY

Ray likes to tell long, prickly stories
of porcupines, hedgehogs and mice.
As the class leans in with rapt interest,
he whips out worms, bedbugs and lice.
We squirm when he talks about green goo in guck –
we beg him to please, please stop!
But Ray is just getting started –
no halting the King of Pure Shock.
He'll gross out his classmates on show-and-tell days
when he slips off his shoes and proudly displays
nail fungus, toe jam, a plantar wart split in two:
He boasts that the wart
has worn a hole
in his shoe.

When our teacher Miss McShinn can take it no more,
she faints straight away on our clean classroom floor.
When she awakes, Ray promises
in his big, toothy grin,
no more to tell tales
that would knock out McShinn.

And that was the last time
the class ever heard
about bugs, Ray's feet
or even green goo –
since his stories moved on...
to the reasons
pond scum
smells like moldy
beef stew.

rigamarole: n. confused, rambling, foolish or meaningless talk

CURIOUS KABEEL

"Good night, Kabeel," said Papa Hasid.

"Papa?
If I walk backward instead of forward,
will eyes grow in the back of my head?"
"I guess you can ask your mother, Kabeel,
then skedaddle off into bed."

"Is a hiccup the opposite of a burp?"
Curious Kabeel asked his mother.
"That is an answer I do not know,
perhaps, go ask your brother?"

"Brother Bart, if I go to bed early,
will morning come earlier, too?
Will Time push itself forward?
Could I grow older than you?

"...and if the sky has a limit,
then where does outer space end?
They look the same, so at the end of space,
does a new sky begin again?"

"Kabeel, my brother,
keep asking questions
no matter how simple they sound.
A question unasked or unanswered
veils a truth that may never be found."

OLD GERMS' Lyrics

Just sittin' round hangin' down
drippin' offa dirty faucets....

Old Germs—
like to
congregate, change their shape, imitate,
simulate, infiltrate, emaciate, incubate,
annihilate New Germs.

Old Germs
love to sit-in-wait, emulate,
instigate, infuriate, penetrate, inculcate,
stimulate, propagate
Good Germs.
Old Germs....

So children, wash your hands both early and late,
or else you'll find your foregone fate
will be to rhyme the suffix "ate,"

...unless, of course,
Old Germs
resuscitate.

OLD GERMS

Jill Clark

Old Germs Just sit - tin' round han-gin' down Drip-pin' of - fa dir - ty fau - cets...

Old Germs like to con - gre-gate, change their shape, im - i - tate, sim - u - late

in - fil - trate, e - ma - ci - ate, in - cu - bate, an - ni - hi - late New Germs. Old Germs

love to sit - tin - wait, em - u - late, in - sti gate, in - fu - ri - ate, pen - e - trate, in - cul - cate,

stim - u - late, prop - a - gate Good Germs. Old — Germs...

Score by Steliana Hindalova

"Old Germs" Definitions

congregate: vb: to gather together into a group

imitate: vt: to reproduce or recreate as a sample or in a pattern

simulate: vt: to copy or follow an original – sometimes in an effort to trick or deceive

infiltrate: vb & vt: to cause a liquid or other entity to permeate an object's pores or interstices [a gap or break]

emaciate: vt: to cause to become thin, or to reduce or to lose flesh or substance

incubate: vt: to help with, create or cause the development of something

annihilate: vb: to destroy forcefully and completely

emulate: vt: to try to become equal to, or to try to excel

instigate: vt: to pester, provoke or goad to move

infuriate: vt: to make extremely angry

penetrate: vt: to pass into or through

inculcate: vt: to teach or influence by reminders and repetitions

stimulate: vt: to function as a physiological awakening to

propagate: vt: to effect or cause to influence in area, size or in number

FACELESS

I flung around and slung around
and spun in place...
when I finally stopped my spin,
I could not find my face.

BODY, MIND AND SPIRIT

Fingernails protect our fingers.
Toenails protect our toes.
Eyelids protect our eyeballs,
but what about our nose?
Our nose cleans the air we breathe
traveling to our lungs.
Our skin and tissue shield the body—
our muscles, veins and tongues.

But what keeps our feelings safe,
our emotions and our hearts?
What we say and how we speak
safeguard those hidden parts.

emotions: n. a personal reaction such as fear or anger that may further
cause physiological alterations and sometimes changes in behavior

The Mushy Green Bean RECIPES

57

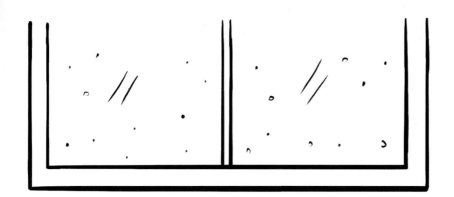

HOLIDAYZIE

CHESTER VALENTINO

Chester strode a lonely path–
a quiet, soft-souled sort.
His tongue seemed clogged, his throat in knots,
his lacings tied athwart.
To run or amble, or even stroll
caused Chester pained attention.
Head over heels for Mary Gait–
too afraid his love to mention.

Her eyelet's blue with an inner soul
toe-tapping to be asked,
one day the hopeful Chester
fell at her feet and fast.
But Mary Gait did not kneel down
to lift his lowly carriage,
as from her feet a fragrance killed
all hope of love and marriage.

athwart: adv. the opposite of the expected course or layout

carriage: n. posture, or the characteristic way one carries or comports the body

corpse flower: n. an arum-family tropical herb whose reddish-violet interior smells like rotting flesh. [Mary Gait's bonnet and illustrated background resemble the corpse flower.]

Valentine's Day, February 14

WHOSE NAPTIME?

How many stories
will Mom read me?
How many pages
till Mom's asleep?
How many books
till I hear a snore?
When I slip off the bed
and out the door –
into my bookroom
to go read more.

National Reading Month, March

JANIS MCMANNIS

Janis McMannis wished her name didn't rhyme.
When people asked her – her name,
she'd say, "Another time."
But these people pursued her –
wherever she'd go –
screaming, "WHAT IS YOUR NAME?"–
(like they didn't know).

Janis McMannis changed her name
once and for all –
to Mary McClary McNary McFall.

National Poetry Month, April

MISSOURI SUMMER NIGHTS

Dear Patrick, Shannon, Molly and Kevin:

Do you remember our stars?
Five freckled faces gazing in awe...
sleeping on a sand-tarred deck above the garage.
Glad God finally turned out the lights.
Dazzled by the galaxy's sway,
the midnight-drop from the roof,
prized apples wriggled from the Johnson's trees,
yellow Delicious stuffed next to Red.
Proudly pajama-bagging them home.
Satin strawberries sneaked from the Lowell's forbidden patch,
their hound's lone, warning howl—
the flight through the persimmon path,
persimmon pulp smashed between naked toes,
the scrambling lattice climb to the roof,
five saucy smiles tucked beneath a loving Dipper.

National Siblings Day, April 10

65

THE CHILDREN'S TREE

The old oak tree invites Shanice
to a stairway bound by leaves:
"Please, feel my trunk's limber branch
and climb with eager knees.
Perhaps you'll try to reach and see
how high you'll go today
shedding spindly limbs to earth
in eager, curious play.
Glance quickly at my robin's nest
and marvel at her eggs....
Peer beneath a millipede
and count its many legs.
See the squirrel watching you
...tail whipping all around?
Observe a single file of ants
marching to the ground.
The red and black ladybug
when you hold her high,
wings sprout out from her shell
before they stretch and fly.
A caterpillar humps along
in slow and metered grace,
antennae guiding it until
a moth will take its place.

National Arbor Day, final Friday in April

"Shanice, the sun is falling fast...
and you must scamper home.
But tomorrow...
the leaves and moss and acorns
will share stories
of their own."

Rustling leaves flap and sing a song into the wind.
A tree awaits each childhood day to entertain its friend.

MY LITTLE GREEN TRUCK

I took my green truck everywhere,
with many a scrape and a crack.
I put grass and dirt and piles of rocks
upon its sturdy back.
But then I drove my trusty truck
through golden-green wet lands,
and after that, my little green truck
rusted in my hands.

Wetlands exist for myriad birds,
the otter, bobcat, and mice.
Little fish hide in the rushes
from their bullies late at night.

What does not belong in a wetland?
Purple loosestrife, trucks, trash and roads.

Help the mink, muskrat and beaver
retain their natural abodes.

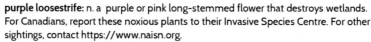

purple loosestrife: n. a purple or pink long-stemmed flower that destroys wetlands. For Canadians, report these noxious plants to their Invasive Species Centre. For other sightings, contact https://www.naisn.org.

World Environment Day, June 5

LETTER-HATCHING

The first letters of some words in soft sounds speak and flow,
starting with inviting vowels like "a" "e" "i" "u" "o":
On an airy afternoon,
an ant ascends a tree –
the aero ant
alights aloft –
a flying ant is he.

Then bleating, blathering, bamboozling "B's"
push the vowels aside,
but again sneak in the diphthongs
where vowel sounds group and glide:
Can you say the word "oil"
and hear the "o" and "i"?
I bet you'll hear them blended
as in "boil" when you try.

alliteration: n. a close connection of similar consonant sounds. Alliteration creates a musical effect and may enhance a point, mood or particular meaning
Example: Barry beat the blueberries in a half-baked shell. [Did Barry beat the blueberries vigorously, or lightly? The "b" sound in this sentence connotes a bit of a more earnest whipping of those berries]

assonance: n. a close connection of similar vowel sounds occurring at the beginning or middle of a word. Assonance is used to create a rhythmic cadence, dramatize a mood or create an emotional effect
Example: "You'll glimmer and glitter and gloss as you glow, to flitter and flutter and sprinkle like snow." from "The Bubble Machine" *Loose Balloons* book

consonant: n. a letter used in English that does not include the vowels, a, e, i, o, u, and sometimes "y" and "w"

diphthong: n. a speech sound created when two vowels occur together and are pronounced by blending the two sounds of each vowel to create a unique monosyllabic sound
Example: How loud can a cow shout in a crowd?

National Literacy Month, September

VAMPIRE TREATS

Zombies and ghouls troll the night,
one time a year to shock you a'fright.
Hug your friends close as you trick-or-treat,
or a ghoul might swoop down
and try you to eat....

Not YOU silly,
or your good friend Mandy.
No!
Ghouls on Halloween
crave Halloween candy.

Halloween, October 31

74

WEST INDIAN MANATEE

Warm ocean or a quiet bay
  will lull this gentle giant
as she lolls and rolls to sway
  among the many grasses of the sea,

Contented Manatee.

Grazing, gracing languidly
in underwater fields of weed,
  munching leisurely
with little need,

Sacred Seacow.

Who adopts an orphan calf as if her own,
  but squeals and squeaks and screams if
baby's lost alone,

Protective Manatee.

Lover of the temperate sea,
  Mermaid to the Ancients,
wallowing in shallow shores,
  ocean reefs
and coral floors,

Friendly Manatee.

Asks nothing of our earth
  but to browse and nibble water greens,
our legendary Siren of the Sea,

  Peaceful Manatee.

National Manatee Awareness Month, November

76

TURKEY JAMBOREE

Turkey baked in giblet stew,
mashed potatoes gravied through,
cranberries swimming in a sauce,
fruit salad fluffed and lightly tossed.

Please don't think me base or rude,
this poet's pun on festive food:
This jamboree of food seems blessed
all because a bird got dressed!

Thanksgiving, fourth Thursday of November

DOLLY THE CHRISTMAS DOG

Admiring lights one Christmas Eve, driving to and fro,
as Santa waved from rooftops — his reindeer grazed on snow.
We came upon a little dog shivering in the sleet.
This tiny dog sat whining on the cold and pebbled street.

"Stop the car," screeched Ellah, "before you hit that dog!"
Two points of light like tiny eyes
misted through the fog.
This lonely little puppy would not leave the road that night.
She sat straight up in the street, her eyes now stars of light:
"I'm going to find my home tonight," her sad eyes seemed to say,
"my belly aches with hunger, and someone's lost my way."

Still, the dog would not come near us,
and ran into the night;
two days we searched the woods for her — no puppy came in sight.
But three-long-days later
(we had never given up)
ran trotting from the woods
a black and tawny pup.

Christmas Eve, December 24

79

Straightway she leaped into our car,
a shivering, freezing pup,
just happy for a family
who had never given up.

Today, Dolly is my service dog, she guides me where to go.
When I get lost, she leads me through rain and sleet and snow.
At home, Dolly talks to us,
she chatters up a storm,
she cuddles with her best friend Nel,
so safe, so loved, so warm.

THE BLACK-CAPPED CHICKADEE

The loveliest bird to hear
in Northern Christmas climes
is the black-capped chirping chickadee
singing –
two-note
winter songs.
The trees this small bird tweets from,
the conifer, spruce and pine
warm our living rooms and windows
twinkling love at Christmastime.

black-capped: adj. the top of the head looks like it is wearing a black hat or cap
chickadee: n. a small North American song bird that often appears to have a dark
head or a cap-appearing-like structure

Christmas Day, December 25

82

ONE FOR THE ROAD

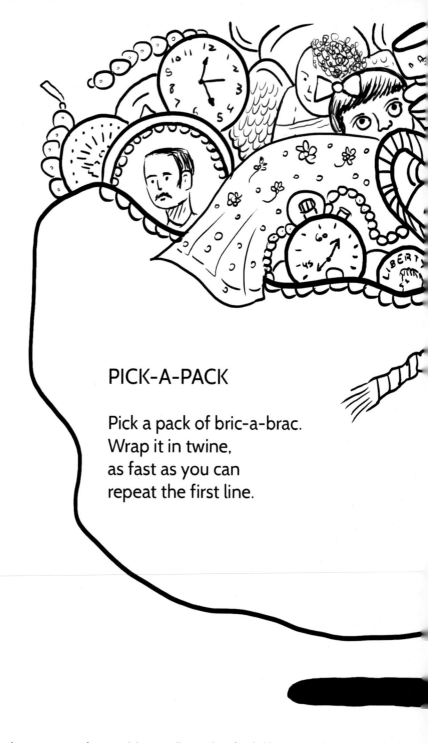

PICK-A-PACK

Pick a pack of bric-a-brac.
Wrap it in twine,
as fast as you can
repeat the first line.

bric-a-brac: n. a variety of memorabilia or small items that often hold sentimental or ornamental value

APPENDICES
A, B, C

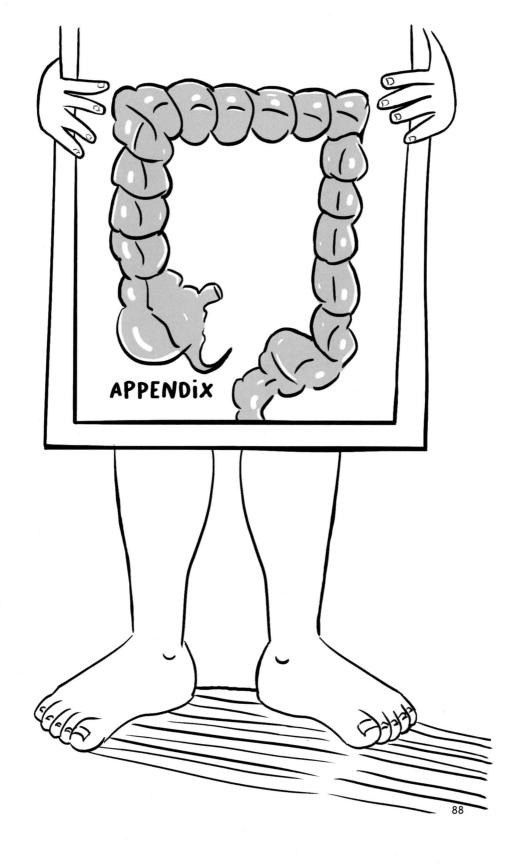

APPENDIX

APPENDIX A
CREATIVITY TWISTERS

APPENDIX A,1.

WRITING ACTIVITIES

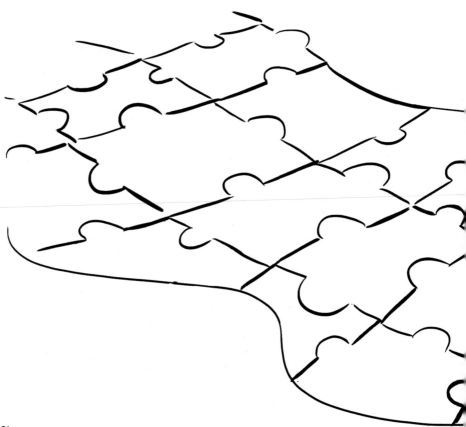

APPENDIX **A,1**.a. *Sunburst*

What would you title Ireland's drawing?

I like the title *Sunburst* because it appears that when the child looks up toward the sky, butterflies release and a burst of colors pattern themselves.

Please write as many titles for this drawing as you would like:

Ireland Williams
Age 11

APPENDIX **A.1.**b. *Bus-O-Rama*

Write a 25-word story or an eight-line poem inspired by Ellah Hawkins' illustration: Have fun titling your writing.

Ellah Hawkins
Age 10

APPENDIX **A,1.**c. *Seashell*

Write a poem or story to go with the drawing.
If you prefer, you may title your creation after you
complete your poem or story.

Vivian Saad

APPENDIX **A,1**.d. *Old Toy Car*

Which poem title in this book do you think inspired Ryan's car drawing? Create a story or poem of your own inspired by Ryan's drawing.

Ryan Morgan Hawkins
Age 9

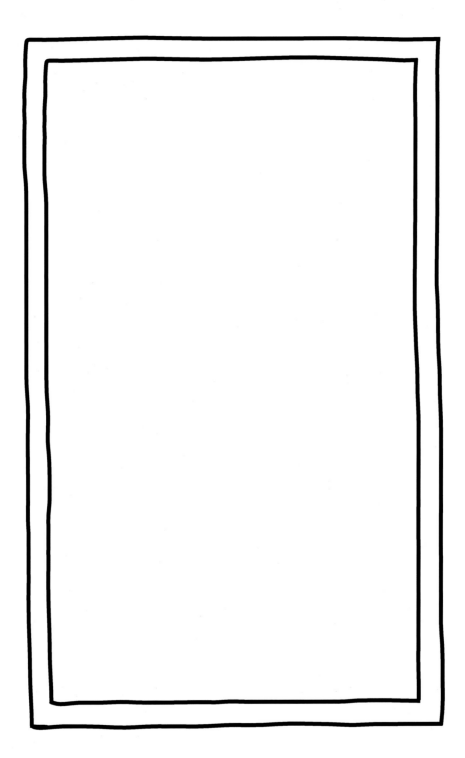

APPENDIX **A,1.**e. *Bird-Nesting*

How about writing a poem or short story inspired by Vivian Saad's illustration below?

APPENDIX A,2.

DRAWING AND/OR WRITING ACTIVITIES

APPENDIX A,2.a.

Draw in the book or on your own paper a cloud picture. To create the poem below, Patria Hawkins Slaughter sat down in the grass in her front yard, looked up at the sky, and wrote out this poem:

HOT AND WET CLOUDS

Clouds are not always in the sky.
Sometimes they melt from the sun,
or when it rains...
they get soaked to earth....
Be careful,
you might be walking on a cloud.

Patria Hawkins Slaughter
Age 7

APPENDiX **A,2.**b. Toad Puzzle Line Drawing

Without lifting your pencil or crossing any lines, draw one continuous line from where the toad sits to where the frog awaits.

Brandy Winston

APPENDIX **A,2.**c.

Below is a sample graphic form from which you can either <u>draw in characters</u> and/or <u>create dialogue and plot.</u> See the Graphic Design Contest Guidelines listed on the author's website: www.jillswriterscafe.com.

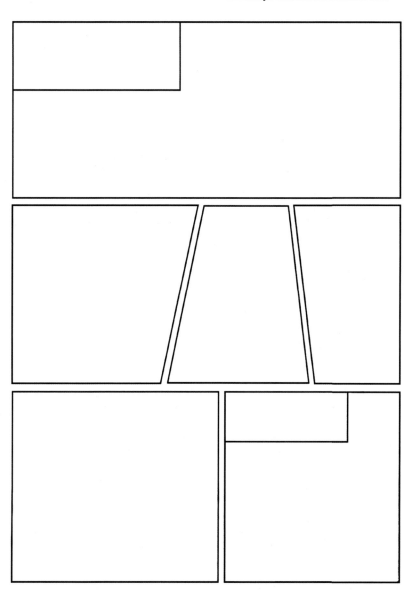

APPENDIX A,2.d.

Please write a "THINGS I DON'T LIKE" poem, or a "THINGS I DO LIKE" poem. Illustrate or draw pictures that show what you like or do not like.

THINGS I DON'T LIKE

I don't like...
Broken pencils
Dead animals
Books with easy words
Things that are dirty

Ellah Hawkins

THINGS I DO LIKE

I like...
to hear frogs croaking from a pond
to watch a stream rush over gray pebbles
to feel the soft powder of a moth's wing
to smell a new-born rosebud

Jill Clark

APPENDIX A,2.e.

OKRA

Named okra, lady's fingers, kingombo and such...
I care not, as I don't like you very much.

Shannon Morgan

OKRA'S APOLOGIA

Please!
Try me, try me, try me,
in my most delicious way.
Have you ever mixed old okra
in soupy-slop souffle?
Try me, try me, try me
in a cherry-chocolate sauce.
As an after-dinner treat—
my strings make sturdy floss.
No need to love your veggies
to love the likes of me.
I'm classified as "fruit"
as tasty as can be.

Jill Clark

apologia: n. a defense

Would you like to draw your own companion poems or write two poems that connect to one another in some way?

companion poems: n. two poems that relate to one another by expressing two points of view, or defending, completing and/or enhancing the idea set forth in the original poem

APPENDIX B

THE STORIES BEHIND SELECT POEMS

"The Centipede" came about because as a child growing up in Missouri, we picked up logs to discover insects and snakes. I found shy millipedes. They drew up to almost a ball. They slowly reopened as if to say "I trust you." Because we were careful, this version of millipede never sprayed its defensive hydrochloric acid on my brother and sister and me. Because of the differences in insects and the locals you will find them in, do not touch any insect unless you know what it is, and even then, it is best to let them pass by unharried.

Millipede

But our parents warned us to recognize a centipede when we saw it because of its poison. Also, centipedes are unusually fast, not prone to balling up, and they make it clear with their agile speed-of-escape that they do not want to be handled. In the poem "The Centipede," I mention sixty feet to unlock the stereotype of people assuming centipedes have 100 feet, since "centipede" etymologically means "one-hundred-footed." In reality, depending on the species, these arthropods have either less or more than one-hundred pairs of legs. The house centipede looks much less fearsome than the giant red-headed centipede we found outdoors in Southern Missouri. These large, bright red-heads serve as a natural wonder, and if you see them, you will know not to hurt them or hold them; just be grateful that you were able to view such a magnificent creature.

Red-headed centipede

If you find the house centipede (pictured below) in your bathroom, remember, they eat cockroaches, silverfish, bedbugs, moths, and spiders.

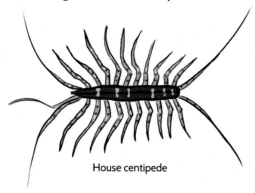

House centipede

"The Shy Rainbow Snake" idea intrigued me because biologists and herpetologists had classified this coy snake as extinct. Recently, however, this "moccasin eel" reptile was identified in Florida, and a reward is being offered (at the time of this book's first printing) if someone can document this painfully shy snake. The snake beneath the poem is of the subspecies *Farancia erytrogramma seminola*, and is thought to have a darker belly, perhaps predominately black. The common rainbow snake *Farancia Erytrogramma* may have a more colorful belly–pink or red. Because of the rare sightings of the shy rainbow snake, this information is believed to be correct, but not absolute.

Common rainbow snake *Farancia Erytrogramma*

The European mink (below) has been reported as extinct. Perhaps this large semiaquatic, carnivorous mammal possesses a means of self-preservation like the rainbow snake? I hope so.

In North America, the gregarious otter's habitat is directly affected by the number and water quality of the American river streams. The abundance of our water sources must be protected. Polluting aquatic habitats not only influences the health of marine mammals, bio seagrass, and other semi-aquatic and aquatic animals, but also directly affects the health of humans.

"Story Clouds" drifted its way into my mind when aboard a jet plane from Florida to Missouri. I had taught a unit of Greek mythology to highschoolers, and as I gazed past the piercing rays of sunlight streaming through spunky cumulus clouds, I noticed the heroic shapes resembled Zeus and Apollo poised in battle. The idea of these two ancient, fictional characters jousting in midair perhaps speaks to you in a similar way when you read about Thor, Captain Marvel and Iron Man? My superheroes derive from not only Greek Drama, but also from Welsh and English Arthurian Folklore (see p.38's poem "My Cousin's Drawing").

"The Hiding Place" resulted as a metaphoric piece — inspired by the African-American poet Paul Laurence Dunbar's poem "We Wear the Mask." Unfortunately, and coincidentally, COVID-19 and its variants came about in our world after the writing of "The Hiding Place." In the psychological sense, sometimes we have to figure out when it is safe to let down our masks.

"How to Handle a Bully" erupted as the final poem that I wrote for this book. Anyone at any stage of life can be bullied.

As I penned this poem, having been blindsided by a bully, I had to step back and figure out why and how it happened? I tried most of the researched anti-bullying devices listed in the poem. But because my provoker possessed a particularly powerful vantage point, only two of the recommendations ultimately worked.

"**Jimmy Defy-Ya**" — zanily outlandish, reminded me of certain students I had taught in my high school classes, and the scenario reminded me of myself, since I have ADHD. At times, it can be incredibly difficult to sit still (unless day dreaming): A quiet classroom can be a torture chamber — and truly listening? — the Grand Torture Master.

"**Rigamarole Ray**" reigns supreme as *Where Do Balloons Land's* gross-out poem. After all, what is a children's poetry book without the "rub" as Shakespeare dubbed it. For further explanation, allow me to digress to the most revolting account from the first book in the series *Loose Balloons.*

In that mostly socially appropriate book, do you remember another *ad nauseam* piece entitled "Billy Bales"– *who likes to chew his nails all the way down to the quick?* That story blossomed as a result of one of my students – who sat on the front row (a foot from my desk) – gnawing his nails back and forth as if eating a buttery-boiled corn cob. And as I remember correctly, a variety of slurping sounds accompanied his mid-class snack. Rather than heaving my stomach contents though, I hyperbolized (exaggerated) his food fest by creating the lyrical account "Billy Bales."

My ability to withstand regurgitating behaviors came about because of my older brother Patrick's efforts to see what it would take for his younger sisters to stop pestering him. But more than anything, I tried to sustain Pat's shocking verbal suggestions, because if I could act like they didn't bother me, at age six, I could tag along with him to explore the secrets of insects and animals hidden in the woods.

From across a culvert, Pat and I would ogle a beaver busily constructing a dam, or view brown bats hanging upside down in the Missouri caves. When we came upon a blue-racer snake, Pat would catch it and hold it up marveling that this wavy shape exceeded my height – while its deep-blue glistening sheen denoted a serpentine reptile of great muscular strength. Then Pat would find a ring-neck snake and cradle it in his palm as if it were a baby worm.

He even captured snakes and put them in cages; we would catch and feed them their natural diet, and then he would release them back into the wild. Pat's dream of becoming a veterinarian did not come true. But he educated the neighborhood kids concerning which snakes not to bother, and which snakes that they could have as pets.

A child needs a forest or even some untended acreage to experience the freedoms of nature, and to learn to respect the divine ecological interchange that takes place within.

Blue-racer

Ring-neck

"Curious Kabeel" came about as a tribute to the longest-residing sultan in the Ottoman Empire: Suleiman the First, also referred to as Süleyman the Magnificent. Although not historically blameless, he wrote poetry to his wife, instituted laws that saved lives [his people and sometimes his captors'], encouraged the designs of buildings that influenced both the Eastern and Western architectural styles of his day, and overall emerged as a sultan who possessed an enlightened sense of leaderful purpose. As a result, Suleiman helped create and influence The Golden Age of the Ottoman Empire.

"**Old Germs**" presented itself to me one day as a tune while intently scouring a bathroom sink. I imagine that routine but necessary scrubbing has provoked many-a-painstaking ditty.

Fortunately, the former opera singer and musical expert Mrs. Steliana Hindalova converted this country twang into a musical score. Thankfully, today, we know more about the chameleon character of injurious germs.

The "**Holidayzie Chapter**" includes seasonal poems. And although Kwanzaa and Hanukkah are not designated as winter holidays, their celebration dates occur close enough on the calendar to cause confusion. With that in mind, we wanted to include Kwanzaa candles to show our respect for the development of a date for an African-American celebration of life. Because Juneteenth became a United States Federal Day of Observance in 2021, one year prior to the copyright of this book, I wanted to indicate appreciation for a formal Juneteenth honoring as well.

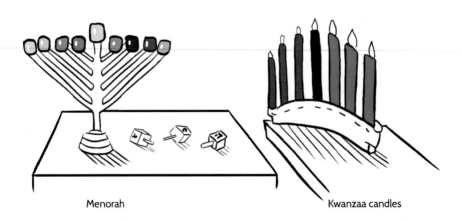

Menorah   Kwanzaa candles

"**Chester Valentino**" sprung forth as an extended metaphor. Did you catch the comparisons of two things in the poem that are essentially unalike? I hope that you had a laugh at the end of the poem.

When the comparison of one thing to another maintains a thematic or concurrent aligning of similar objects or ideas all the way through the poem, then that juxtaposing is referred to as an "extended metaphor."

In "Chester Valentino," can you identify which words-per-line indicated the likening to a shoe?

Moreover, in "Chester Valentino," the literary similarities toggled between two characters — Chester Valentino — a shy boy and accompanying awkward shoe — and Mary (Merry) Gait — a more outgoing, romantically hopeful girl.

Did Vivian Saad's tennis-shoe anatomy help you to perceive the various parts of a shoe punned to create the story of Chester and Mary's short-lived and ill-fated relationship?

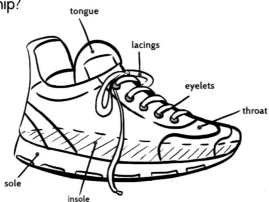

Teachers: A list of over twenty words punned on the shoe and characters are listed on the author's website.

"Whose Naptime?" rolled out when I thought back to my mother's efforts to read to her five young children during naptime. Often, she was so exhausted that she fell asleep before finishing the books. Studying the pictures and letters during mom's unintentional catnaps fostered my continual curiosity and relationship with words.

"Missouri Summer Nights" recounts the series of events that I underwent in the hot, steamy summer evenings of our beloved, verdant state of Missouri. These nightly ventures were enhanced by my brother Pat cleaning and emptying two-used soup cans. He hammered a nail into the middle of each of the two soup-can ends. He threaded the end of a string into the hole of the one can, and then threaded the other end of the string through the hole in the other. He knotted the string on the outside of each can so that the string ends would not pull back through.

Then we talked into the hollow tin-plated containers to our neighbors next door (the string extending from where they slept upstairs to where we slept on our flat-garage roof). This taut, cotton string placed between the two soup containers acted as a sound-wave conductor that carried our voices back and forth.

There are a number of examples of how to create this home-made audio device on social media. Have a parent or responsible guardian assist you in this fun endeavor.

I wrote **"Missouri Summer Nights"** to preserve our childhood portrait of freedom and innocence. Please understand, though, that I am not recommending this nocturnal activity for children, only chronicling what my siblings and I experienced at this historically safer time.

"Dolly the Christmas Dog" turned out to be a ballad because the story details how we discovered our chihuahua-miniature pinscher mix, Dolly. Our granddaughter Ellah sees well from a distance. And if Ellah had not screamed that Christmas Eve when she saw this black-and-tan puppy on an unlighted street, and Ireland my other granddaughter had not pointed precisely to it, I would not have slammed on the brakes in time to stop the car.

The beige and white dog that you see in the poem is Nella (her fur the color of a vanilla bean). We found Nella one afternoon lost in Florida — frantically sniffing back and forth on a cracked patch of dusty road. We thought we had rescued a hairless dog. With medical shampoo applied nightly, each following morning, we were happy to discover, like the miracle on some commercial terra-cotta seed-growing vases, the wonder of new hair growth. When no one claimed ownership of Nella, she joined our family. Because of her docile nature, Nella calms our frisky Dolly.

During school-learning activities, when I present the ballad "Dolly the Christmas Dog," our dog Dolly likes to "chatter up a storm" for the kids with her high-pitched, ear-blasting yodeling.

APPENDIX C
ANNOTATED WORKS CITED AND LESSON PLANS

Jill Clark presents online lesson plans guided by the most recent educational standards that align with her books *Loose Balloons & Where Do Balloons Land?* Contact Jill if you would like for her to present a children's activity to enhance your curriculum: **jillclark2write@gmail.com**

Review the sources below from **various websites, teachers, researchers and authors that relate to select poems from the book.** [Request permission from the site publisher or author/s to use in your classroom if the site does not directly state that the lesson plans are free or can be used without permission.]

"The Centipede"

The Missouri Department of Conservation. "House Centipede." Missouri Department of Conservation publisher, 2021, https://mdc.mo.gov/discover-nature/field-guide/house-centipede.

3rd Grade Lesson Plan

"Centipedes and Millipedes." Better Lessons. 2020, https://betterlesson.com/lesson/644747/centipedes-and-millipedes.

The **"Shy Rainbow Snake"** has been documented in Fisheating Creek in Glades County, Florida and is believed exclusive to that area. To learn more about this particular reclusive snake, contact the herpetology staff at the Florida Museum of Natural History, Division of Herpetology, University of Florida, Gainesville, FL. https://www.floridamuseum.ufl.edu/florida-snake-id/snake/rainbow-snake/.

For additional information concerning the rainbow snake, access https://www.biologicaldiversity.org/species/reptiles/South_Florida_rainbow_snake/index.html.

Iñigo, Zuberogoitia, et.al. "Facing Extinction: Last Call for the European Mink." 1 May, 2018. (*Mustela lutreola*). *Annals of Reviews and Research.* Vol. 2 Issue, Juniper Publishers, 2021, https://juniperpublishers.com/arr/pdf/ARR.MS.ID.555581.pdf.

Manville, Richard, H. "The Extinct Sea Mink, With Taxonomic Notes." Proceedings of the United States National Museum. The Smithsonian Institution, Washington D.C., 1966. Vol. 122, https://repository.si.edu/bitstream/handle/10088/16923/USNMP-122_3584_1966.pdf?sequence=1&isAllowed=y.pp.1-11.

National Wildlife Federation. "North American River Otter." National Wildlife Federation, 2021, https://www.nwf.org/Educational-Resources/Wildlife-Guide/Mammals/north-american-river-otter.

"Wishing-Star Wait" Questions

1) In theory, how would you measure how far your wish would travel? [We measure distance to stars in light years.]
A. What is a light year?
B. How far does light travel in one year?
C. How far does light travel in one day?
D. How much time will pass during one light year?

2) A. If you made a wish on a star, how far would the closest star be to you?
B. In theory, how long would it take for your wish to arrive at the wishing star and return again?
C. What is the star's name?

3) Why make your wish on just a single star, when several would be more fun? A series of stars in a pattern is called a constellation. The Little Dipper is a constellation that we can see almost every night directly overhead.
A. How many stars are in the Little Dipper?
B. What is the famous star at the end of the Little Dipper's handle called?

4) The following graphic portrays the Milky Way Galaxy where our sun is located.
A. Can you put an "X" on the following picture where the sun should appear?
B. Can you draw a small stick-figure, or place one where you think the character making the wish in the poem is located? [hint: The earth is near the sun.]

Teachers and Readers: For more lesson-plan questions that align with this book, and to find the answers to the "Wishing-Star Wait" questions, access the following: **www.jillswriterscafe.com**.

Check in the menu bar for "Lesson Plan Questions for *Where Do Balloons Land?*"

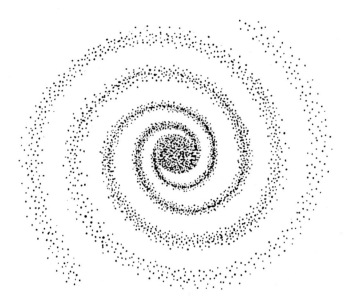

John Clark
high school chemistry and physics instructor

"The Hiding Place"

Dunbar, Paul Lawrence. "We Wear the Mask." Paul Laurence Dunbar. *We Wear the Mask: Complete Poems of Paul Laurence Dunbar.* New York: Dodd, Mead and Company. *Poetry Foundation,* 2021, http://www.poetryfoundation.org.

Turpin, Zachary. *Twilight is their Child. Uncollected Poems, Letters and a Short Story.* University of Idaho. 2018. Resources for American Literary Study. Penn State University Press, 2018, Vol. 40. pp.152-158. The Pennsylvania State University, 2019, https://doi.org/10.5325/resoamerlitestud.40.2018.0155.

"We Wear the Mask" Lesson Plans for High School Teachers

This plan includes standards, length of the lesson, and course objectives. [Check to make certain that you are using the school system's updated state standards.]

Gray, Kerry. "We Wear the Mask Lesson Plan." *Study.com,* 30 May 2017, Study.com, 2003-2021, study.com/academy/lesson/we-wear-the-mask-lesson-plan.html.

"Jimmy Defy-Ya" Lesson Plans for Kinetically Active Students

Instructors: View these 20 teaching gems to help students pay attention and enjoy reading while accommodating varied learning styles:

Kluth, Paula and Kelly Chandler-Olcott. "A Land We Can Share: Teaching Literacy to Students with Autism." "20 Ways to Adapt the Read Aloud in the Inclusive Classroom." 2007. *Reading Rockets.* WETA Public Broadcasting, 2021, https://www.readingrockets.org/article/20-ways-adapt-read-aloud-inclusive-classroom.

"Curious Kabeel" Lesson Plans for teaching Suleiman the Magnificent

Discover an interesting website (below) to introduce students to Suleiman the First.

"Suleiman the Magnificent Biography for Kids." *Ducksters.* Technological Solutions, Inc., (TSI), 2021, https://www.ducksters.com/searchducksters.php?q=Sulieman+the+Magnificent.

Middle School Teachers might find interesting the following CBA (Classroom-Based Assessment) Lesson Packet for Sultan Suleiman:

Luhrs, Rebecca. *The Golden Age of the Ottoman Empire Suleiman the Magnificent*. Office of Superintendent of Public Instruction. Jan. 2005. "The Dig Deep Classroom-Based Assessment." World Affairs Council. CBA Lesson Packet for Middle Schools. 29 Jan., 2008, https://currikicdn. s3-us-west-2.amazonaws.com/resourcedocs/5bc8ad1fbfbab.pdf.

High School and College Resources: Author's Note
[Blackwell's articles require usage permissions.]

For more in-depth information concerning Süleyman the Magnificent, Blackwell Publishing archives scholarly articles for high school and college students.

Below is a well-documented dissertation with an impressive list of primary sources. Keep in mind that a dissertation proclaims a researched position on the subject by the writer, and another dissertation by a different scholar may defend an alternate point of view on the same subject.

Yelce, Nevin Zeynep. *The Making of Suleyman the Magnificent: A Study of Process/es of Image-Making and Reputation Management*. Sabanci University. 2009, PhD history dissertation, https://core.ac.uk/ download/pdf/11742467.pdf.

"Holidayzie Chapter"

"Celebrate Kwanzaa in the United States." *Scholastic Inc.*, 2021, https:// www.scholastic.com/teachers/lesson-plans/teaching-content/ celebrate-kwanzaa-united-states.

"Chanukkah Curriculum Updated." Limudei Code-Esh. *An Intermediate Scratch Jr. Coding Curriculum Integrated with Jewish Education. Coding as Literacy Approach*. Tufts University. Tufts UP. DevTech Research Group. 2020.

Croteau, Jeanne. "17 Ways to Celebrate Juneteenth with Kids." *We are Teachers*. 15 June 2021. https://www.weareteachers.com/ teaching-juneteenth/.

"Kwanzaa-What is It?" Akwansosem African Studies Program. *Outreach Newsletter for K-14*. University of Wisconsin-Madison Vol. 3: 2. March 1990, https://www.africa.upenn.edu/K-12/Kwanzaa_What_16661.html.

"The West Indian Manatee" is Florida's official state marine mammal.

Sadly, the high rate of manatee mortality at present is from manatee injury by watercraft, but mostly because of loss of seagrass. Seagreens are the manatee's main food source, and because this verdant aquatic grass is so scarce now, the manatees are starving to death.

Additionally, toxic water has contributed to the demise of sea and river biomass. Cleaning the water is critical to the seagrass regrowing. Without action and collaboration between legislators, concerned citizens, scientists and educators, the future for this endearing, friendly marine mammal is bleak.

Brown, Haley. "Inside the Effort to Save Florida's Dying Manatees." 20 Aug. 2021. Florida Politics. Publisher Peter Schorsch. 2021. https://floridapolitics.com/archives/451730-inside-the-effort-to-save-floridas-dying-manatees/.

If you and your friends can think of a way to help the manatee, please contact The Florida Fish and Wildlife Commission at 888-404-FWCC (3922), and remember you may also contact one of the world's foremost experts on manatees, the Executive Director of Save the Manatee, Patrick Rose. He can be reached through the following address:
Save the Manatee Club, 533 Versailles Dr., Suite 100, Maitland, FL 32751.
Phone: 1-800-432-5646 or 407-539-0990.

Save the Manatee Club has worked since 1981 to preserve these gentle, endangered marine mammals: www.savethemanatee.org.

Educators, for Save the Manatee Club's virtual presentations visit:
https://www.savethemanatee.org/manatees/education-materials/educator-resources/.

"Disappearing Seagrass Hurting Beloved Manatees in Florida." The Associated Press. 1 March, 2021. Extensive-Enterprises 2021, https://floridapolitics.com/archives/407924-disappearing-seagrass-hurting-beloved-manatees-in-florida/.

Definitions:
algae blooms: n. excessive unicellular algae growth that becomes toxic to waterways, marine mammals, animals, and the humans that depend on them. One of the leading causes of toxic blooms is fertilizer runoff with substances that contain phosphorus.

mortality: n. death, particularly in large numbers.

seagrass: n. called "the lungs of the sea" as this grass releases oxygen in water.

For the definitions, a composite of the following resources consulted...

Collins Online Dictionary

Merriam-Webster's Collegiate Dictionary Eleventh Edition

Merriam-Webster's Online Dictionary

The Oxford English Online Dictionary [Thank you to Stetson University's duPont-Ball Library in DeLand, Florida]

"Are Frogs and Toad the Same?" Wonderopolis HQ. Scholar.Harvard. edu.2020.

https://scholar.harvard.edu/files/adam/files/phonology.ppt.pdf

National Center for Families Learning: Louisville, KY 2014-2020.

Wonderopolishttps://www.wonderopolis.org/wonder/are-frogs-and-toads-the-same#

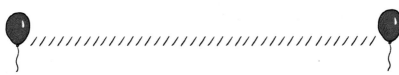

In *Where Do Balloons Land?*, the idea of balloons is used symbolically and metaphorically. In reality, these loosed colorful, festive, helium-filled concoctions are injurious to the atmosphere, marine life, and animals.

Please read "The Damage Balloons Cause" and "Balloon Research" on the author's website to learn more about how popped litter from balloons imperils not only birds and turtles, but works its way into all types of wildlife and waterways. **www.jillswriterscafe.com**

Please consider finding other creative means to celebrate, and if you and your friends can offer healthy alternatives, then we would like to post your ideas on the website. Who knows, you might even write a book about how to protect the environment.

Just think if a balloon could be made out of nourishing, edible, biodegradable material that would augment the lives of animals and the soil?

Jill Clark freelances prose and poetry. She hosts The *Society for Children's Book Writers and Illustrators'* Volusia County online, regional critique group. She retired Professor Emeritus from Daytona State College and currently enjoys working as Children's Educational Specialist for Taylor and Seale Publishing.

As they relate to her poetry books *Loose Balloons* and *Where Do Balloons Land?*, Jill conducts online art and reading activities guided by current standards for public and private schools. Ms. Clark earned a Master's Degree in Reading Education from Stetson University and a Master's Degree in Liberal Studies from Rollins College. Florida Teaching Certifications in English grades 8-12, Reading K-12–along with critical ESOL Endorsements (English Speakers of Other Languages)—enriched the classroom for all of her students. She appreciates speaking at writers' conferences and passing on information that will help others.

Select the Home menu bar from her website at **www.jillswriterscafe.com** to view her "Speaking and Activity Calendar." Contact the author if you would like a reading and/or art lesson plan presented: **jillclark2write@gmail.com**.

Jill's husband John teaches physics and chemistry for Volusia Online Learning in Florida.

Additional literary publications by the author include...

The Henry David Thoreau Walden Woods Project, The Vanishing Series by Lerner Educational Publishers, *THEMA, The Silver Empire, Pocket Change Literary Magazine, Ariel Chart International Literary Journal, Garden Blessings, Guardian Angel Kids Online Magazine, Bumples Online Interactive Magazine for Kids, Shoofly Audio Magazine, Orlando Sentinel, The Daytona Beach News -Journal, The Excelsior Springs Standard, Women's Wilderness, Celestial Musings, Blind Faith Books, Hedge Apple.*

Forthcoming – *The Indian River Review,* and *TallGrass Writers'Guild Play Anthology* published by Outrider Press.

Author's Website

Vivian Saad illustrates children's and young adult books. She has a Bachelor's Degree in Graphic Design from the University Belas Artes of São Paulo, and lives in Brazil. She has illustrated more than forty books and has participated in exhibitions and catalogs in countries such as Argentina and Canada. Jill Clark's middle grade poetry book *Where Do Balloons Land?* is Ms. Saad's illustrating-and-designing debut for a book in a foreign language. Vivian's illustrations capture the emotions and experiences that bond us as humans.

To contact Vivian and view her work visit:
http://www.viviansaadilustras.com

Brandy Winston is a freelance illustrator with over five years' experience in the Children's Book publishing industry. She graduated in 2013 with a BFA from the Cleveland Institute of Art and has since worked to design and illustrate books for both traditional and self publishers. When not working, she enjoys playing video games with her husband and doting on their adopted dog, Luna.

Brandy Winston's portfolio:
https://bwillustration.artstation.com

Illustrations by Brandy Winston:
"Frog's the Name," "Toad's Retort," "Fiddle Dee Dee,"
"Turkey Jamboree," "West Indian Manatee;" Toad Puzzle Activity.

NOTES

If you enjoyed this book, we would appreciate a review.

Made in the USA
Columbia, SC
24 February 2023